Paris in Colour

PARIS IN COLOUR

Introduced by Jacques Prévert
with 109 photographs in colour by
Peter Cornelius

Bramhall House in New York

This edition published by Bramhall House, a division of Clarkson N. Porter, Inc.

German edition © Econ Verlag Düsseldorf 1961

Translation by Jonathan Griffin
and Margaret Shenfield

Colour plates printed in Switzerland by Héliogravure Centrale S.A. Lausanne

Text printed in Holland by Koch & Knuttel, Gouda

Bound by Van Rijmenam, The Hague, Holland

CONTENTS

Blue bird, colour of time, fly to me quickly.

MADAME D'AULNOY

Paris in colour is the title.
Colour of time is this book's colour, and if the blue bird does not
appear visibly he is there all the same, he is there all the time.
Peter Cornelius has had eyes to see him, and shows him to us
with simplicity. Sometimes a child in the grey of a barn, among
the old disused bicycles, mutilated and scalped dolls and brand-new
spiders'-webs, unearths a dusty and torn picture-book.
And the book is many-coloured and the child is lost in wonder.
In his discovery of Paris, Peter Cornelius is like that child.

Paris in colour.
City colours, flashing fresh colours for the foreign traveller, local colours
of everyday, weathered colours, forgotten by the tired inhabitant.

Colours of Paris,
colour of time.
Colour of phantom time, ghostly and very much alive,
unforgettable, indifferent and uncaring.
Of time intact, invulnerable, of time wandering imperturbably
through the promiscuity of the past, of today too, and of
last year, and the next few years still further away in that confined
space where there will perhaps be human animals surviving.
"The colour of time?" says a passer-by. "Don't make me
laugh. One hasn't time to see that clearly, one hasn't time
to talk about that. Might as well discuss the sun with
a squeezed lemon!"

Colour of time.
Man today, on the watch behind his windscreen or standing
on a row of studs between two bumpers, has eyes for two colours only,
two poor policing glows: red and green.
And the exhausted people sitting at the pavement cafés
in the city centre or the suburbs stare, without a word, at
others like them passing by.
An exotic, languishingly passionate gramophone accompanies
that whipped-up, automatic, motorised ballet. And the shouts
of the traffic police, punctuated by obsessive whistle

blasts, sort and unsort, in a wise and exemplary
disarray, the communal transport of the great urban flocks.
And yet, here and there in the city, mysterious islands — condemned
as unhealthy or miraculously spared by the bulldozers
— remain as silent and eloquent witnesses to a past
that is still young and always calm and welcoming.

Colours of Paris.
Utrillo, Lautrec or Fernand Léger colours, when the city
is unwittingly a museum.
Colours of the colour photograph so long decried by
enlightened art-lovers.
Colours of railings, shop-fronts, doors and windows,
waste plots, passages.
Colours of bad taste but life's taste, colours of the taste
of day and of night.
The hues of buildings are not hues of reality. Their paint, whether
it is still wet or has been cracked for centuries, is fresh and violent:
the passers-by see it as in a dream, without ever looking at it; yet,
hung on the shabbiest of their walls and with no shadow of a
signature, it has no need to envy the innumerable
latest masterpieces of action painting, so highly prized.

Colours of Paris.
Colours of the Tuileries, of the Ile Saint Louis and the Quai
de la Mégisserie: turtle-grey and mouse-grey. Colours of
the Canal Saint Martin: ultramarine blue, and ultraterrene,
and the hue of the fair blue Danube when the Danube is blue.
Colours of the Gare Saint Lazare at a quarter past six in
the evening: steel-grey, furnace-blue and smoke-black.
Colours of the four seasons of the Rue Mouffetard at noon:
cherry-red, lemon-yellow, orange-orange, apple-green and radish-pink.

Colours of Paris.
The roofs of the Opéra are green, the Moulin Rouge is red,
and Notre Dame is grey and the Sacré Coeur white. But the Parisian
no longer sees these colours, he is in them all the time.

If he leafs through the volume he finds himself once more
in familiar country, and perhaps it will give him great pleasure.
Peter Cornelius has not looked at the city through the
tourists' key-hole, and the city has been grateful to him
for that, has taken him by the arm in friendly fashion and
led him wherever his own sweet will thought fit.

"The camera is a paint-box but also Pandora's box," the city said.
"Implacable, undeniable, innumerable are the images of
misfortune and misery.

"Leave those in the background. Be kind to me,
don't open the box too wide!

"Show simply my joy in living, in spite of my griefs, my
torments. Show my pretty girls, my care-free children,
those brand-new children on horses that are already old.

"Show the woman with the black shawl and the four white dogs; also
those two other women at the foot of the Tour Saint Jacques, sitting
on a bench with a stone lion watching over them, the one sewing,
the other reading. And the *art nouveau* entrance to that Métro
station, still as modern as ever, and prettier than ever. And
also the last of the Wallace fountains, the one with the four women,
which used to have a tin cup on a chain.

"Show, too, the Rue de l'Ave Maria and the Jardin du Vert Galant
and the Passage de la Petite Boucherie and Alfred Jarry's beloved
Rue de l'Echaudé. And the flea-market, the flower-market
and the bird-market. And show as well, since you insist,
Saint Germain des Prés and Montmartre by night.

"How could I dissuade you from that, I who have so long been
the capital of pleasure?

"But the pleasure has changed, decidedly. My gaiety used
to be wild: now it is psychoanalysed. Formerly, the
lights of evening found me fair and those of night caressed
me with their gaze: now they flash in my eyes, harsh,
greenish, pale and unsteady. On Montmartre my lipstick
is livid, the neon will-o'-the-wisps dance over pancakes
flambées in petrol, and the *poularde demi-deuil* seems to have

come from the grill-room of the *Institut Médico-légal*.

"Luckily the sleep-walking moon still walks my roof-tops.

And the ghost of the sun sometimes laughs aloud.

"And I too laugh like that — I have too much heart and too clear

a head to be always weeping. And I sing constantly,

or very often. Though they've driven away my street musicians.

"I know — I've been told — I was not built in a day.

But what they always forget to add is that one day I might

well be destroyed in a night.

"What would become, then, of my old colours, mingled

with the last gleams of my today?"

Colours of Paris.

Peter Cornelius listened to the city and let her guide him.

In the courtyards, the children of Spring were gathering up

the leaves of Autumn, Winter's prospectus for the great season

of white. And the blue schoolboys and girls of the Place des

Vosges and the black students of the Boulevard Saint Michel

were waiting for the holidays, for the sun and the summer.

Peter Cornelius was going home to Germany and was saying,

"Au revoir" to Paris, just as I was saying "Au revoir"

to Hamburg, a city in his country that cast a spell on

me. But already the colours of that city were those of the

swastika flag. All that is already twenty-eight years ago.

Colours of Paris.

In a deserted yard a poor green plant in a poor broken packing-case

utters a cry of distress, of thirst. Out comes the old woman

with the watering-can, sister to the old woman who feeds the cats

and the old man who feeds the sparrows. And the plant

recovers its colours and calls to her a green "Thank you".

Colours of Paris,

of her secret music, her silent distress, her happy

dreams, her songs of love.

Jacques Prévert

for Dolly

4

RIVE GAUCHE

au seuil étroit

37 GALERIE

37

BOOKS

SEINE

49

ÉTOILE · BASTILLE

MARCHÉS

MONTMARTRE

PARIS

This book was occasioned, and first made possible, by a new type of colour film which I was able to try out in Paris. At that time I did not dare to hope that such a beginning would grow, five years later, into a large volume of colour pictures. Since then the original material has often been changed, but the basic idea — to create a picture in colour of Paris and its people, by means of living, unposed photographs — has been carried through consistently.

Now, the idea of showing the people of Paris in pictures is, of course, not new. Books by Brassaï, Izis, Doisneau and others contain hundreds of splendid black-and-white photographs of this kind. But there was nothing in colour. Could one, in fact, using the potentialities of colour photography, add something completely new to these pictures?

Colour does not of itself improve a photograph. The cluttered quality of random reality, automatically reduced and made abstract in a black-and-white picture, is preserved in a colour picture. Therefore colour photography, if it is to capture the living instant, demands an extremely critical choice of the rare moments when subject, colour and form are simultaneously and convincingly in harmony with each other.

Until recently it has been practically impossible to capture coloured impressions with such speed and directness. The equipment was so dependent on shades of light, brightness and contrasts that it prevented the photographer from concentrating on vision as much as these pictures demanded. With the advent of colour negative film, colour finally ceased to be fortuitous and unalterable. If it had not become possible to correct the automatic impression of the camera at a later stage, the nuance, tone, delicacy, or contrast of colour instantaneously photographed could never have been reproduced.

My first attempts were encouraging. Friends of mine in Paris, who had known and photographed the city for years, were enthusiastic because my pictures recaptured, in colour, the qualities they loved in Paris. And they made me more and more convinced that one day the pictures could grow into a book. I remember in particular the kind judgment pronounced by Izis, who himself has produced the most beautiful books of Paris photographs, and through whom I came to know Jacques Prévert.

Seeing colour as the order and design in the chaos of the big city, in people's movements, in the fleeting change of light, in the transitory quality of shades, reflections and lighting, tempts one to abandon oneself to sheer visual pleasure. The eye becomes, as it were, sensitized, and there sets in a state of increased photographic ability in which one sees everything clearly and as though for the first time. In this condition one begins to react to everything and select things from the general confusion with tremendous speed and concentration.

Colour photography does not mean giving up abstraction, but it does mean a different kind of selective and 'abstracting' vision from that involved in black-and-white photography. Just as the abstraction of black-and-white has been used as a positive quality, so now one makes conscious use of the peculiar characteristics of colour. Rightly used, they can save the picture from the dangers of that all-pervasive realism which black-and-white photography, with its automatic tendency towards abstraction, always avoids.

It was never my intention to take the kind of picture which I could hold up to the subject and compare with it, to decide whether it looked exactly like that. I am not saying that the colours were as shown, but that these colours can be seen if the eye is capable of seeing them. In reality few colours are exactly like this, with this intensity and tone. Even motionless subjects are constantly changing as the light changes; they become colourless, or glow, or are irradiated by bright sunlight, or disappear into the shadows. And in my later work on each photograph I compare it not with the subject, but with my memories, my conceptions and intentions.

It is not only changing light but time which alters the colours of things. A wall may crumble, be cleaned and shored up and painted a colour which will only come to fit in with the street as a whole many years later. It was not so much the unchangeable element as this very transience that I wanted to record in my pictures.

Anyone who is sensitive to colour easily succumbs to the charm of decorative colour and colour detail. A whole book could be made of details of old walls, but it would be little more than a delightful game with colour compositions. (It might also, perhaps, show how many of the basic elements of modern painting can be traced to the streets of Paris.)

It would have been easy, too, to make a book of pictures of the Rive Gauche between the Seine and the Boulevard St-Germain. 'Il faut échapper au charme du Quartier,' I was warned by a Parisian friend when he had seen my many pictures of this district. With colour pictures it seems to be particularly difficult to make an objective choice. And Paris is such an inexhaustible theme that each new book can only be a beginning. You cannot capture the essence of this city systematically, however much its logical plan may suggest the opposite.

To non-Parisians, no city is so identified with a score or so of monuments and places of interest, which occur again and again in almost every book of Paris pictures. Of course, all that is Paris too; Les Invalides, the Eiffel Tower, and the Louvre just as much as the Métro, the Bois de Boulogne, and the Folies-Bergère; the Panthéon, the Arc de Triomphe and the Sacré Coeur just as much as Les Halles or the Place Pigalle. Any comprehensive dictionary of pictures would include them all. But it would be both discourteous and unjust to want to be objective about such a city. So I tried to choose people and streets, squares and markets, colours and things at the precise chromatic moment when something of the essence of the street, and, at the same time, of the city, would be visible in each picture.

Many streets, particularly on the left bank, have so individual an atmosphere that it is possible to capture it in one well-chosen instant. The Rue Cardinale, near the Place Furstemberg, grey with pink carnations. The Quai de la Mégisserie with the bird-shop called the 'Perruche Bleue', one of many. The Rue de Seine in the morning with the subdued colours of its houses and galleries. The Place Jussieu near Les Halles aux Vins in the lunch hour. The Pont St-Michel in the late afternoon, when those hurrying by still have time for admiring glances. The Rue St-Benoit, near St-Germain-des-Prés in the evening, when the small sports cars are out. The Quai des Orfèvres in front of the dark grey of the Palais de Justice. The Canal St-Martin, where the anglers are reflected and the barges disappear under the street into two narrow sluices, only reappearing beyond the Place de la Bastille. To anyone who is familiar with the city the mere names of the streets will be enough to show whether I have captured the characteristic atmosphere and colouring of this part of Paris.

The West, with its broad, heavy avenues, its monuments, visitors and big squares, is reserved, cold. We have at last escaped from 'le charme du Quartier', with its wealth of impressions; here, in the course of hours, one may find only one or two pictures. I often stood in vain before the vastness of the Place de la Concorde, until one evening the sun disappeared behind the obelisk and let the hundreds of lamps shine out over the blue-grey of the shadows.

The Vikings in the Champs Elysées (p. 53) are no less typical than the ostrich standing in a yard in the Rue Jacob (p. 70), because unexpected sights of this kind occur again and again and nobody is any more surprised at them than at, say, the barge full of red wine which amazes foreigners. Only when a celebrity visits the hairdresser's do curious crowds gather, to be moved on by the police. But the great grey monuments are far outside the scope of the eye which is concentrating on close-ups, colouring and life. Sometimes, however, when the great monuments' reflections show between books or jewellery, it is possible to fit them into a picture.

The markets are multicoloured and confused. It is even harder to find some chromatic order in this chaos than it is in the streets. The gay colour promised by the Marché aux Puces is hardly to be found at the Porte de de Clignancourt any more; one must look for it, instead, in October on the broad Boulevard Richard Lenoir at the Foire à la Ferraille which stretches from the Bastille far into the north-west. It still has that absurd, improvised muddle which in the better markets of St-Ouen has long given way to an orderly and expensive refinement. The markets in the Rue de Seine-Rue de Buci and, above all, the Rue Mouffetard, are as colourful and lively as ever; one can only fully experience their southern temperament on a Sunday morning by letting oneself be drawn into the noisy scrimmage all around.

Often the twilight hours of early dusk, when the hard sunlight was slowly fading, were the finest and most colourful of the whole day. The first artificial lights mingled with the blue of the dusk, and even when it was already dark we stood in front of the cafés or in the streets and tried to capture something of the atmosphere of the evening, no longer in short moments but in half or whole seconds.

Even from the technical point of view there is now no longer any real reason to be prejudiced against a small picture-size. Some of the pictures in this book have been enlarged to thirty-nine inches for exhibitions. But above all I cannot react so swiftly and unobtrusively with any other size. As a matter of course, therefore, especially for this work, I used a Leica camera. I wanted to stay as close as possible to reality, so I deliberately rejected the interesting possibilities offered by long focal lengths. The majority of the pictures were taken with the 35 mm. wide-angle lens, although not so much for technical reasons. On the contrary, the special quality of the wide-angle lens — its ability to reproduce many details sharply — is particularly dangerous with colour, and I can only cope with it in snapshots by reacting with great speed and exactitude to every variation. The advantage, as I saw it, was that at such a close distance I was drawn into the action, whereas with the long focal length I was cut off, as though looking through a telescope. This meant not only a different optical perspective but also a different kind of communication.

All the pictures were made on Agfacolor negative film (CN 17 and CN 14) which allowed me to make corrections to the colour, contrast, brightness, and picture-shape in the enlargements. Thus at the moment of taking the picture the technical considerations were no more complicated than in using black-and-white film. To be relieved of such technical worries is particularly important and valuable; for colour makes more intensive demands on the eye, and the crucial moment can rarely be recaptured.

For the first time it has been possible to make a colour book, from the very beginning, in a way that has hitherto only been possible with black-and-white. I began by selecting the pictures from small coloured copies. When once the sequence and the rough sizes had been decided, I made two small black-and-white dummies to scale, and then a book with the colour enlargements in their final size, as a convincing 'manuscript'.

I hope that this book will communicate some of the qualities for which Parisians love their city.

PETER CORNELIUS

LIST OF ILLUSTRATIONS